A NURSERY RHYME PICTURE BOOK

BY

L. LESLIE BROOKE

[ZHINGOORA BOOKS]

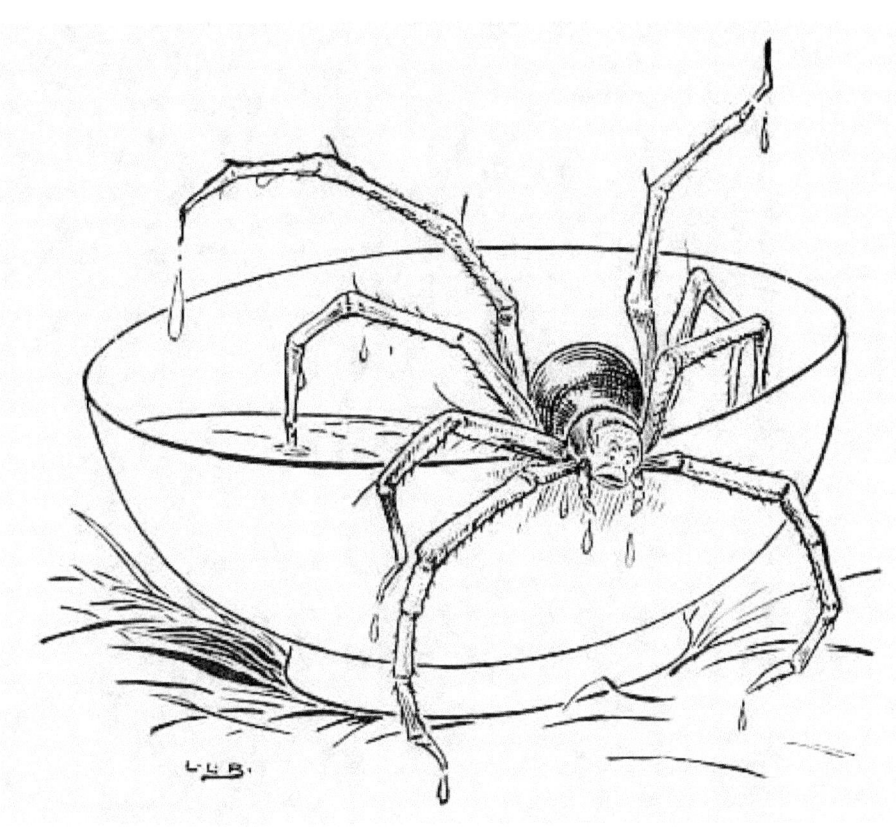

THE MAN IN THE MOON.

THE Man in the Moon

Came tumbling down,

And asked his way to Norwich;

They told him south,
And he burnt his mouth
With eating cold pease-porridge.

TO MARKET, TO MARKET.

TO market, to market, to buy a fat
Pig;
Home again, home again, dancing
a jig.

*To market, to market, to buy a fat
Hog;
Home again, home again, jiggety-
jog.*

There was a man, and he had nought,
And robbers came to rob him;

He crept up to the chimney-pot,

AND THEN THEY THOUGHT THEY HAD HIM

BUT HE GOT DOWN ON T'OTHER SIDE

And then they could not find him;

He ran fourteen miles in fifteen days,
And never looked behind him.

THE LION AND THE UNICORN.

The Lion and the Unicorn

Were fighting for the Crown;

The Lion beat the Unicorn

All round about the town.

Some gave them white bread,
And some gave them brown;
Some gave them plum-cake,
And sent them out of town.

LITTLE MISS MUFFET.

Little Miss Muffet
Sat on a tuffet
Eating of curds and whey;

There came a big Spider

And sat down beside her,

And frightened Miss Muffet away.

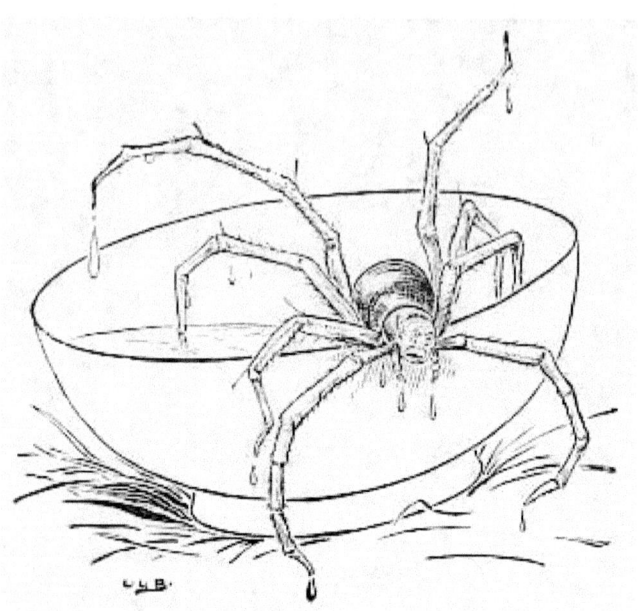

ORANGES AND LEMONS.

Gay go up, and gay go down
To ring the bells of London Town.

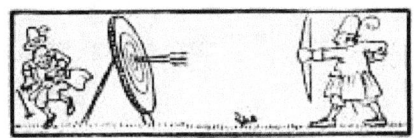

Bull's eyes and targets,
Say the bells of St. Marg'ret's.

Brickbats and tiles,   Pancakes and fritters,

Say the bells of St. Giles'.   Say the bells of St. Peter's.

Two sticks and an apple,
Say the bells at Whitechapel.

Halfpence and farthings,
Say the bells of St. Martin's.

Oranges and Lemons,
Say the bells of St. Clement's.

Old Father Baldpate,

Say the slow bells at Aldgate.

Pokers and tongs,
Say the bells of St. John's.

Kettles and pans,
Say the bells of St. Ann's.

You owe me ten shillings,   *When I grow rich,*

Say the bells at St.   *Say the bells at*
Helen's.   *Shoreditch.*

When will you pay me?   *Pray when will that be?*

Say the bells at Old
Bailey.   *Say the bells of Stepney.*

I am sure I don't know,
Says the great bell of Bow.

Here comes a candle to light you to bed,
And here comes a chopper to chop off your head.

GOOSEY, GOOSEY GANDER.

Goosey, Goosey Gander,

Where shall I wander?

Upstairs, downstairs,
And in my lady's chamber.

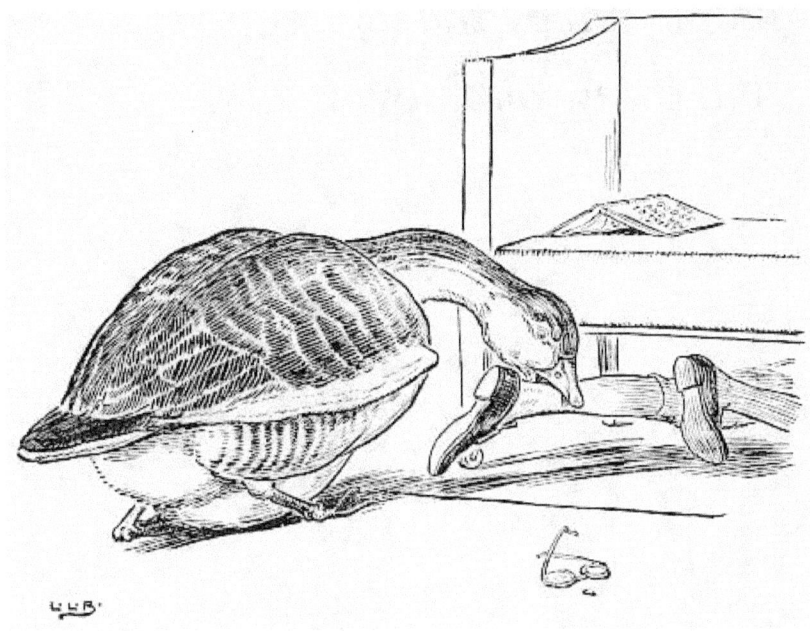

There I met an old man
That would not say his prayers:
I took him by the left leg,
And threw him downstairs.

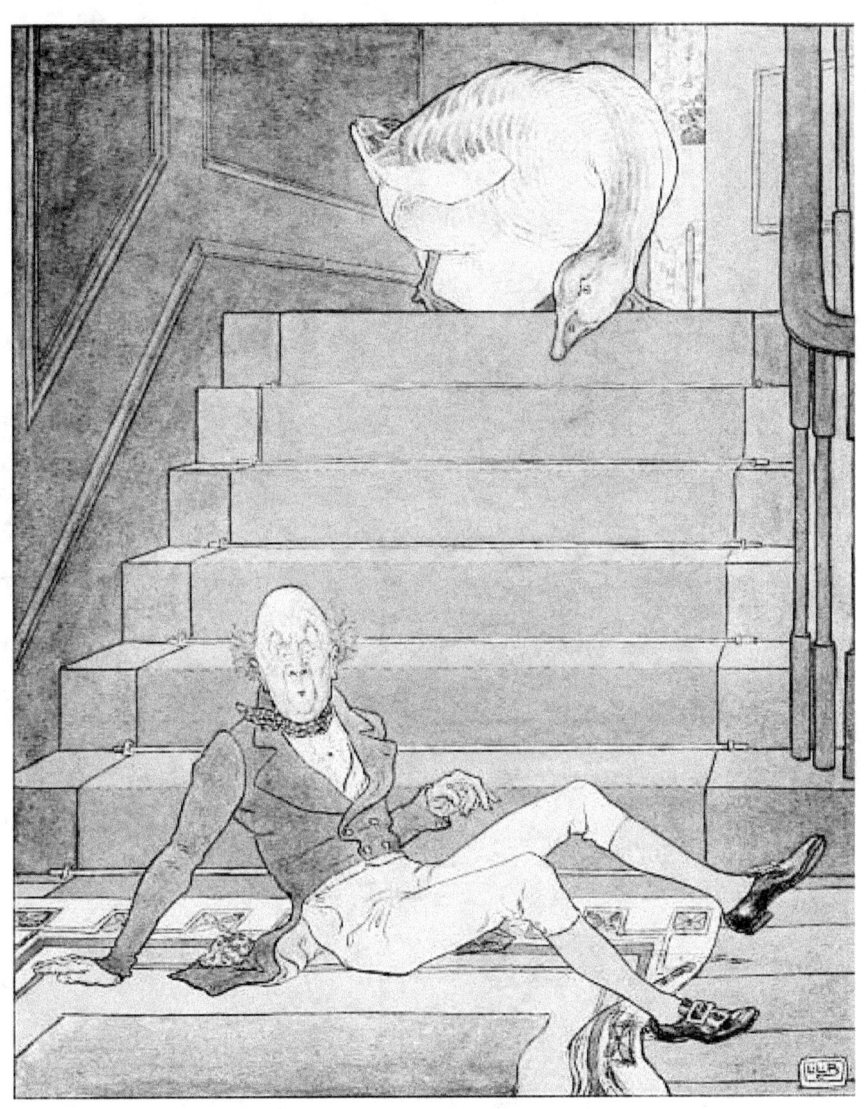

HUMPTY DUMPTY.

Humpty Dumpty sat on a wall;

Humpty Dumpty had a great fall;

All the King's horses and all the King's men
Couldn't put Humpty Dumpty together again.

BAA, BAA, BLACK SHEEP.

Baa, baa, Black Sheep,

Have you any wool?

Yes, marry, have I,

Three bags full:

One for my Master,
And one for my Dame,
And one for the little boy
That lives in the lane!

THE THREE WISE MEN OF GOTHAM.

Three wise men of Gotham
Went to sea in a bowl:

If the bowl had been stronger,
My song would have been longer.

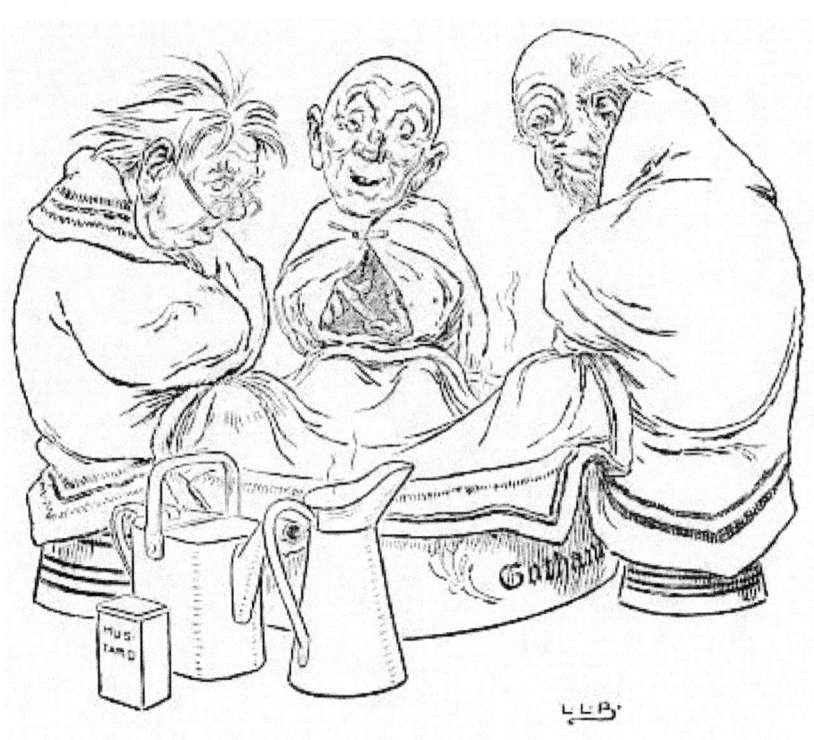

The End